BROUGHT TO YOU BY
TIFFANY ALICHE | THE BUDGETNISTA

@2016 THE BUDGETNISTA

Hey hey hey Dream Builder!

I'm so happy that you've decided to take your finances & life to the next level.

This notebook will help you to make the most of the Live Richer Academy.

I look forward to your success!

Live richer,
Tiffany Aliche

Tip Sheet!

Welcome to the Live Richer Academy (LRA), Dream Builder! I've created this tip sheet to help you make the most of your investment.

- Tiffany "The Budgetnista" Aliche (LRA Founder)

LOG IN
Go to **www.liveracademy.com** and click LOGIN, then sign-in using your email & password.

ACCESS YOUR COURSES
When you log into the Academy, you're automatically taken to the "My Courses" page. You can also click the "My Courses" tab at the top of the Academy.

TYPES OF COURSES
- Prerecorded: These courses have shorter videos and longer, written course materials. They also include a quiz at the end of each course.
- Live Courses: These courses are held live every week. The videos are longer and the written course materials are shorter. There is a quiz at the end of each course.
- Ask the Expert: These live, video lessons are held on Sundays. These lessons follow a Question & Answer format. During these lessons you'll have the opportunity to interact live.

GETTING STARTED
1. Write down your top 3, finance and life goals. (use the goal sheet provided in your Academy notebook)
2. Review the available courses and identify the courses in alignment with your goals.
3. Commit to starting one course and taking at least one lesson per week.
4. Join the Academy forum.

JOIN THE PRIVATE ACADEMY FACEBOOK FORUM
Log into the Academy, then click "Academy Forum" in the menu. Request to join. After sending a request, if your FB name and your Academy name are different, please share both names with us via the "Contact" tab.

USE THE ACADEMY FORUM:
Ask questions, get feedback and encouragement while taking your courses. Also, connect with other Dream Builders and many of the course instructors there. Have a question? Tag an instructor in your post.

Frequently Asked Questions.....

I missed a live lesson, now what? The recordings are made available the same day under your "My Courses" tab in the Academy.

How do I get updates? Every Monday Tiffany will email you the links to all of the live lessons for the week and share any Academy news.

I have a course or "Ask the Expert" lesson suggestion. If you have a suggestion, share it via the "Contact" tab in the Academy or in the Academy Forum.

How do I connect with an instructor? Each lesson contains the instructor's contact information. You can also find many of them in our Academy forum.

ADDITIONAL SUGGESTIONS & TIPS:

- Find an accountability partner in the Academy Forum and check-in with them weekly. Every Wednesday, the Academy Team helps to pair Dream Builders looking for a partner.

- Pace yourself. The Academy is like a library. The courses are your books. Read one "book" at a time. You can check them out whenever you want. You can also re-read any "book" you want.

- The "Ask the Expert" lessons held on Sundays, they are also recorded and can be found in the "Ask the Expert" course in the Academy, under the "My Courses" tab.

Questions? Comments? Concerns? Suggestions? Go to www.livericheracademy.com and click "Contact". My team and I would love to hear from you.

– Tiffany "The Budgetnista" Aliche

BELOW, WRITE DOWN YOUR
TOP 3 *finance & life* GOALS

_____

_____

_____

_____

_____

_____

MY COURSES

Use the following pages to take notes during each

Live Richer Academy lesson.

NAME OF COURSE:

INSTRUCTOR NAME:

Live Richer!

Live Richer!

Live Richer!

NAME OF COURSE:

INSTRUCTOR NAME:

Live Richer!

Live Richer!

Live Richer!

NAME OF COURSE:

INSTRUCTOR NAME:

Live Richer!

Live Richer!

TODAY IS *always* A GOOD DAY TO START.

-ELISE BROWNING

Live Richer!

NAME OF COURSE:

INSTRUCTOR NAME:

Live Richer!

Live Richer!

Live Richer!

NAME OF COURSE:

INSTRUCTOR NAME:

Live Richer!

Live Richer!

Live Richer!

NAME OF COURSE:

INSTRUCTOR NAME:

Live Richer!

WINNING TAKES *work.*

-TIFFANY ALICHE "THE BUDGETNISTA"

Live Richer!

Live Richer!

NAME OF COURSE:

INSTRUCTOR NAME:

Live Richer!

Live Richer!

Live Richer!

NAME OF COURSE:

INSTRUCTOR NAME:

Live Richer!

Live Richer!

Live Richer!

NAME OF COURSE:

INSTRUCTOR NAME:

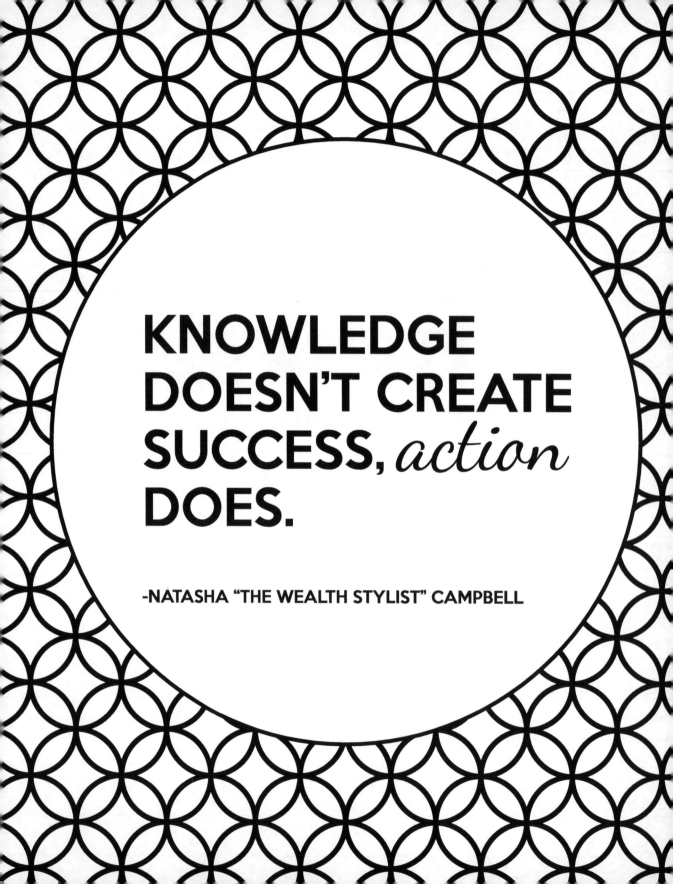

KNOWLEDGE DOESN'T CREATE SUCCESS, *action* DOES.

-NATASHA "THE WEALTH STYLIST" CAMPBELL

Live Richer!

Live Richer!

NAME OF COURSE:

INSTRUCTOR NAME:

Live Richer!

Live Richer!

Live Richer!

NAME OF COURSE:

INSTRUCTOR NAME:

Live Richer!

Live Richer!

DON'T WAIT FOR THE NEXT THING, *make* THE NEXT THING HAPPEN.

-BANANA GEORGE

Live Richer!

NAME OF COURSE:

INSTRUCTOR NAME:

Live Richer!

Live Richer!

Live Richer!

NAME OF COURSE:

INSTRUCTOR NAME:

Live Richer!

Live Richer!

Live Richer!

NAME OF COURSE:

INSTRUCTOR NAME:

Live Richer!

DO WHAT YOU CAN, UNTIL YOU CAN DO *more.*

-TIFFANY ALICHE "THE BUDGETNISTA"

Live Richer!

Live Richer!

NAME OF COURSE:

INSTRUCTOR NAME:

Live Richer!

Live Richer!

Live Richer!

NAME OF COURSE:

INSTRUCTOR NAME:

Live Richer!

Live Richer!

Live Richer!

NAME OF COURSE:

INSTRUCTOR NAME:

Live Richer!

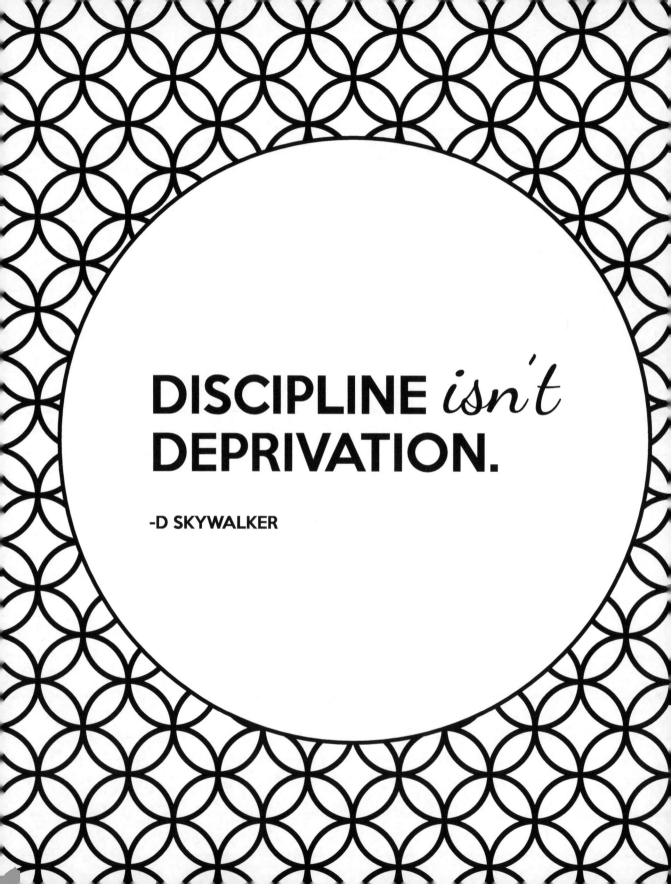

DISCIPLINE *isn't* DEPRIVATION.

-D SKYWALKER

Live Richer!

NAME OF COURSE:

INSTRUCTOR NAME:

Live Richer!

Live Richer!

Live Richer!

NAME OF COURSE:

INSTRUCTOR NAME:

Live Richer!

Live Richer!

Live Richer!

NAME OF COURSE:

INSTRUCTOR NAME:

GRATEFULNESS ACTIVATES *abundance.*

-TIFFANY ALICHE "THE BUDGETNISTA"

Live Richer!

Live Richer!

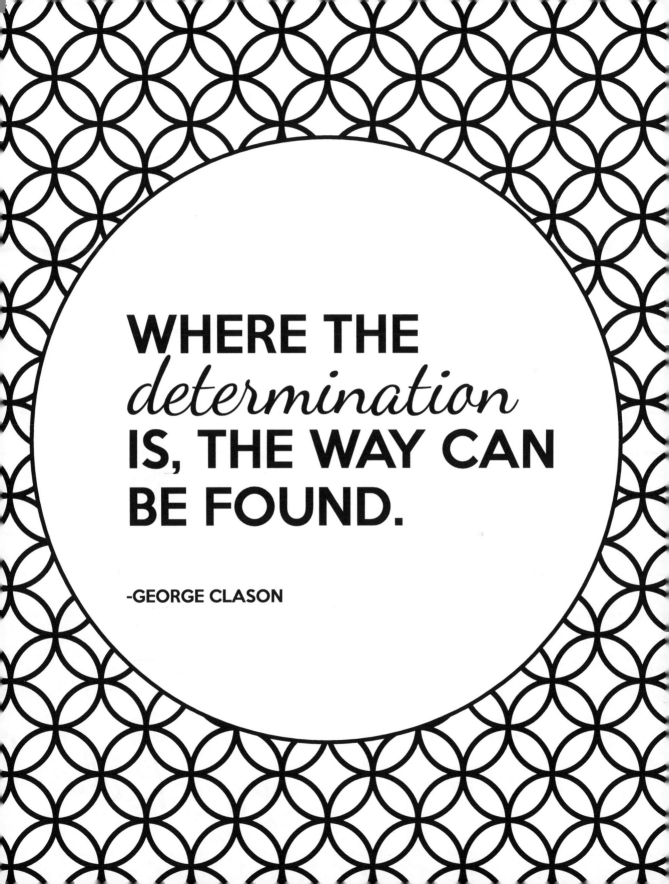

WHERE THE *determination* IS, THE WAY CAN BE FOUND.

-GEORGE CLASON

Live Richer!

ASK THE *Expert!*

Use the following note pages to prepare questions & take notes during each "Ask the Expert" lesson.

Live Richer!

Live Richer!

Live Richer!

Live Richer!

Live Richer!

Live Richer!

Live Richer!

Live Richer!

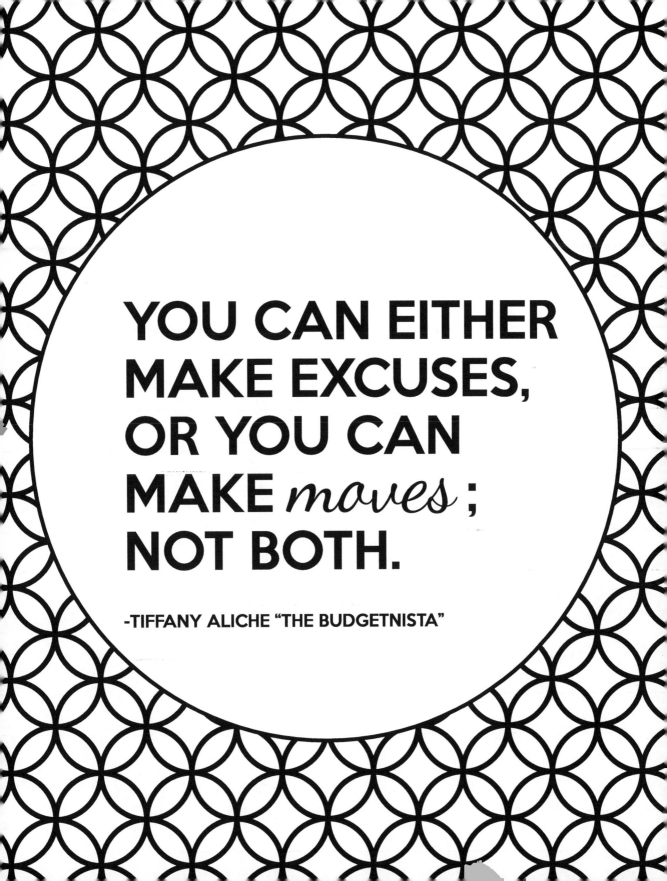

YOU CAN EITHER MAKE EXCUSES, OR YOU CAN MAKE *moves* ; NOT BOTH.

-TIFFANY ALICHE "THE BUDGETNISTA"

Live Richer!

Live Richer!

Live Richer!

Live Richer!

Live Richer!

Live Richer!

Live Richer!

IT'S MORE THAN MONEY, IT'S A *movement.*

-TIFFANY ALICHE "THE BUDGETNISTA"

Live Richer!

Live Richer!

Live Richer!

Made in the USA
Charleston, SC
21 June 2016